Body Language Blueprint

Learn How to Analyze People, Understand Human Behavior and Boost Confidence through Social Awareness

Introduction

Welcome to the book, *"Body Language Blueprint: Learn How to Analyze People, Understand Human Behavior and Boost Confidence through Social Awareness."*

At the pinnacle of social media and online communication, the ability to analyze people and read human behavior is becoming a lost art. Do you know what happens when a necessary ability becomes more and more scarce? Its value increases. I present to you the body language blueprint. It's your turn to possess an extremely valuable skill set. It's your turn to have the edge and be treasured.

Why bother about body language? What is the need? After all, do we not already know enough about body language? Are the body language cues not obvious enough? Can't we already discern if somebody is comfortable or uncomfortable, happy or sad, excited or mellow just by looking at them? Why bother?

The reason is that by going ahead and making an effort to master body language, you immediately give yourself a chance to nurture a skillset of not just taking in other people's body language and analyzing it correctly, but also sufficiently controlling your own body language.

This way, you steadily develop into what some refer to as a 'communicator with intent.' You will cease to be somebody who leaves his or her communication to chance and become someone who takes control of how he communicates and interacts with other people.

This book will teach you everything you need to know about body language. You will learn how to make immediate analysis and come up with correct conclusions, with regard to other people's displayed body language. Better yet, you will know what to do to project the correct body language for whichever situation you are in, as well as the proper responses to give with regard to specific body language expressions.

Respective authors own all copyrights not held by the publisher.

The information herein is offered for informational purposes solely and is universal as so. The presentation of the information is without a contract or any type of guarantee assurance.

The trademarks that are used are without any consent, and the publication of the trademark is without permission or backing by the trademark owner. All trademarks and brands within this book are for clarifying purposes only and are the owned by the owners themselves, not affiliated with this document.

Table of Contents

Conclusion

The Need to Understand Body Language

In the recent past, there has been great emphasis placed on understanding body language. But, why is this the case?

1. **At least 60% of all communication is usually non-verbal in nature**

First, researchers disagree with the 60% figure. Some of them say the true figure is 93%, while others settle on 65%. Either way, they prove our point with even more vehemence. If you insist on only taking verbal communication to heart and ignoring everything else, you are missing a lot. You will never be a good communicator, let alone a great one.

You need to pay close attention to facial expressions as well; to motions of the body, tonality, involuntary motions and proxemics (how close/far a person is from you). We will cover this latter one in depth, in a separate chapter.

2. **Understanding body language is often the first step to beginning and maintaining great friendships**

Well, you may not care to make friends, which is fine really if that's your thing. But if you are keen on making friends or even just improving your existing friendships, then you need to understand body language to communicate effectively and understand what others are trying to communicate.

Let's assume that a good number of people who meet you either withdraw or project some hostility toward you. You may be good-looking and even smell nice on the daily trip to work. But still, the people you meet almost always grow cold, and most of your relationships never seem to progress from the first encounter.

The usual assumption for most of us is that there is something inherently noxious about us, or that most of the people we meet are shallow or perhaps uninterested in us. But oftentimes, the truth is that your body language has a cold edge to it and more so, your body language assessment skills are terrible, so that your responses seem insensitive or detached.

Once you understand body language, you can fix such problems very quickly. It becomes easier to make new friends. Maintaining friendships ceases to become an overly difficult task. As some might put it, you eventually become a 'natural.'

3. **Understanding body language positively impacts your dating skills**

Once you build body language comprehension, it becomes easy to tell if somebody is interested in you. Quite a number of people miss out on dating and even marrying great people because they were unable to read body language that indicated the other person was interested.

4. **Understanding body language helps in maintaining and growing your marriage**

A marriage where one or both parties has poor comprehension of body language is usually doomed, and a major reason why divorce rates in the US stand over 50% is because the current generation is far too obsessed with technology and 'fast' stuff to properly learn old-fashioned stuff like body language and how to interact with people.

For example, when your wife says, with a slightly raised voice, "Josh, or Honey?" then it could be her way of saying "I'm getting ready to ask a favor of you" or "We need to talk for a bit." If your body language skills are proper, you will adjust mentally to the situation and the ensuing interaction will flow smoother. The same is not the case for those who have no clue about body language.

5. **Positive body language skills are a massive help with regard to increasing your confidence**

As you become smarter at reading other people's body language and catching cues, you will ultimately feel less and less anxious about what you can expect in social situations. You will almost always know what to expect before it happens to you. This preparedness and ability to predict interactions will breed confidence in a way few things do. You will be in control and you will know it.

I hope you now know why it is critical to learn and understand body language. Let us now move on to some surprising facts about body language.

5 Surprising Truths about Body Language

Thanks to such TV shows as Lie to Me, as well as countless others which feature 'body language experts, multiple misunderstandings have accumulated with regard to body language. You see, these 'experts' micro-analyze every little thing, and you come off thinking they are perhaps more interested in making body language look like some kind of deep science than actually imparting real education. Here are some surprising truths when it comes to body language.

1. A lot of what experts tell you is just plain wrong and often absurd

It boggles the mind why experts keep perpetrating factoids on how specific gestures have specific, cast-in-stone meanings. It's almost as if every human being is not completely different to another. Gestures are mostly ambiguous; they can mean many things or mean nothing at all. If somebody crosses his or her arms, it could well be that they are defensive, and a bit put off... or it could be they are just cold and want to feel some warmth. But experts will insist that folding arms automatically signals defensiveness and a lack of attraction. I remember attending a party with friends where I met a beautiful woman. We were sharing great conversation and showed each other many signs of attraction. However, about halfway through, my close friend decided to pull me aside. He needed to tell me that he could see she was not interested simply because she had her arms crossed during our interaction. I laughed and shook my head at how ridiculous his observations were as he spoke in my ear. Long story short and for the sake of keeping this book on the right track of virtuous content, let's just say, he was wrong.

Don't judge these people too harshly though; the misunderstanding usually comes from the pressure to come off as definitive and to provide instant analyses, and the history of body language as we know it. Once you combine these two elements, you end up with the sort of rigid assertions body language experts double up on. It may help to listen to them since there's usually some truth to some of what they say, but always do so with a pinch of salt. Just because they don't mean to lie to you doesn't mean they aren't doing it either.

2. The face is quite a poor starting point for reading body language

By the time most of us are all grown up, we have become thorough experts at masking our feelings... at least as they show in the face. We have spent years and years learning to get along and make concessions, so we pretend to be immersed in interactions; we pretend to beam in delight when we feel something entirely different within.

Certainly, we are not completely perfect at executing these polite deceptions. A stray yawn will fail to be sufficiently stifled. But mostly, the face is often a polite mask that helps everybody get along.

3. **The face at times does give away our most potent feelings**

If you learn quite a bit about body language, you can easily pick up micro-expressions: these are sudden, prompt leakages of genuine emotion through the deceptive mask that is the human face. Note that these are very fleeting in nature and they only last a split second. Thus, it takes considerable work to know how to pick up on them. Typically, they only show up when you are hiding a very potent feeling that clashes with what you are admitting to. The genuine feeling will flash across the face and will then be gone.

4. **Body language usually signals intent and not specific meaning**

Here's another one that experts get wrong so often. What body language often conveys, and with great accuracy too, is emotional intent. There are psychologists who believe that whatever a person feels first shows up in their body and only later does it show in their conscious minds. And by later, we mean nanoseconds later. Thus, if you are impatient, angry, hungry or happy your body will register these feelings first and it will signal them. When you learn how to read other people's body language, you become an expert at understanding other people's intent, as opposed to specific meanings housed in their conscious minds.

5. **You are way better at picking up body language cues of people familiar to you than any expert anywhere**

For people you know, you are surely a seasoned hand with regard to reading their body language. Just think about this for a bit. Unless you are an utterly clueless person with no self-awareness, then you know already when your fiancée is angry, your kid is bored or the boss wants something done! With people we know, we have already amassed many, many hours of study. We can tell the signs from a mile away.

Before we move on to actually learning about body language and reading various non-verbal clues, let us learn some mechanics of understanding body language first.

How to Read Body Language

We will start our discussion on how to effectively read body language by learning something about the feet.

Nonverbal Cues of the Feet

This may be a bit of a surprise to you, but it is true that the one body part that can and will reflect what a person is thinking with the highest level of accuracy is the feet. This is why it is important that you observe the feet of the person you are interacting with as close as you can without going over the top.

The theory behind this is that the human feet, along with the legs of course, have been our main means of reaction to threats within the environment for millions of years. The human brain was thus so wired that whenever a threat was faced, the body part that would react first would be the feet. Your feet are the one body component that initiate the fight-or-flight mechanism, and this is achieved either by helping you get away from the danger or fight the source of danger if flight is not a viable option.

Thus, the next time you observe a person, rather than going the usual route of observing them from head to toe, do the opposite and examine them from the feet up.

Feet Direction

The most predictable nonverbal human behavior is turning toward those things or people that interest us, or that arouse a liking for them in us. This is an almost automatic response, and it is often an effective indication when you are determining if another person is happy to see you or would like to be left alone.

When two people are interacting, they usually speak toe to toe. If you notice the other person is turning their feet away from you slightly, or they are repeatedly moving a foot in an outward arc, rest assured that they would rather be elsewhere.

Crossed Legs

Crossed legs, unlike crossed arms, are often a comfort indicator. It is true that people will rarely cross their legs if they are uncomfortable. We cross the legs when we are confident; and confidence walks hand in hand with comfort.

Going back to our theory on brain wiring, the human brain long ago picked up that crossed legs reduce balance, at least while standing, and it becomes harder to react or protect yourself in case you are threatened. This is why the limbic brain only allows crossing of the legs when we are feeling safe.

Let us now move on to reading our torso.

Nonverbal Cues of the Torso

With regard to the torso, we can foretell that the limbic brain will, with great diligence, instruct us to protect this particularly vulnerable part of our body. The torso, in addition to being more vulnerable to serious injury, houses multiple vital organs such as the liver, lungs, heart and stomach system.

When the brain picks up on danger, regardless of whether this perceived danger is real or not, it automatically sends a message to the torso so that the internal organs are shielded from harm.

And this is the main way in which we are able to decode nonverbal torso cues. The 2 primary ones are the 'torso lean' and the 'torso shield':

The Torso Lean

Like the rest of the body, your torso first reacts to danger by creating as much distance between itself and the danger as is possible. When somebody hurls some missile at you, way before you think of intercepting it, your first reaction will be to dodge it. When a person is in close quarters to an obnoxious person, they automatically lean away.

It is very easy to pick up on two interacting people's connection just by looking at how their torsos orient to each other; how they connect. If they are seated near each other and have no qualms about ventral fronting, there is a very high chance that they share a very good connection and relationship.

The Torso Shield

When people try to shield their torsos somehow, you can almost be sure that there is some discomfort in place.

Men, perhaps because they possess stronger, harder physiques, will torso-shield in very subtle ways. A man might mess around with his watch, pull at his shirt sleeves, fiddle with his tie or lightly scratch his chin stubble. These are subtle protection forms that will communicate that the man is a bit uneasy.

On the other hand, women shield their torsos in much more overt ways. Most of the time, a woman will cross her arms over her belly in an attempt to protect the torso and feel safer.

With this latter one, here is a tip for men reading this: If you are on a first time date with a woman and she exhibits this kind of nonverbal behavior, do not panic. Most of the time, it doesn't mean that she does not want to be anywhere near you. It often is the case that she feels intimidated by you, especially if you are a bit older/more accomplished, and thinks that hurt or rejection is a true possibility. A great way to dissipate this uneasiness is to ask them to high-five; a move that promotes comfortable feelings while exposing the torso.

Let us now decode the arms, which are also a critical part of understanding body language.

Nonverbal Cues of the Arms

The arms are a bit of an underappreciated body part with regard to the evaluation of nonverbal behavior. Too many people rely on facial expressions or nonverbal cues of the hands and fingers to help them investigate the substance behind a person's actions and reactions. The arms, however, are great in revealing significant information with regard to a person's actions.

The theory goes that during the evolution process after people began to walk upright, arms were unnecessary for movement and thus were able to be deployed to assist us in other ways.

From lifting heavy things to launching us off the ground and providing defense, the usefulness of the arms became more diverse as it moved away from its primary use of movement. The freedom associated with the movement of the hands and arms allows them to be very responsive whenever threats are encountered.

The two most interesting nonverbal cues of the arms are 'the regal stance' and the 'arms akimbo.'

The Regal Stance

This is the move where we place our arms behind our back. Think of those noblemen in movies, especially when they are addressing others.

This move is often associated and observed in individuals possessing a high status. It is a move, which signifies distance, and the intent to seek this distance so as to convey personal value.

However, this move is often badly interpreted because it communicates that the person 'owning it' does not fancy being touched. And as we know, people detest it when they feel unworthy of touch, seeing as human touch is very vital for our interaction.

With this in mind, as a species, we have learned to employ touch as sort of a barometer of our present feelings. Where arm-distancing is in place, you can bet real money that there is some discomfort in place; we tend to keep our arms away from those things that we dislike. Think of a baby diaper; you will use as few fingers as you can to remove it and will most likely dispose it as fast as possible.

Arms Akimbo

Our arms may be used as territory-marking tools, and by the way despite our very advanced social nature, humans are territorial creatures at heart. Establishing territory and protecting it was a matter of life and death hundreds of thousands of years ago, and the human mind, as it evolved, never lost sight of this.

Perhaps, the most significant and potent territorial display projection is the 'arms akimbo.' This is the move that has you place your arms around your waist, and it may be used to either establish dominance, confidence or communicate some 'issue' to other people.

If you are addressing someone and they adopt this pose, it is very often the case that they have an issue with something you said, or are getting wound up and will soon be confrontational.

Nonverbal Cues of the Hands and Fingers

Considering all animal species, the human hands are unique in the sheer volume of things they can accomplish. In fact, every invention that called for detail and concentration was created using the hands and fingers. Hands can catch, grasp, poke, scratch, punch, sense, feel, assess and mold the world and the things in it.

In addition, they are the perfect tool for self-expression. The hands add an edge and intensity to our conversations; they add energy to interactions and they are great tools for helping others understand and unscramble the messages we have for them.

And needless to say, the hands can indeed betray intentions and they are very good reflectors of subtle behavioral nuances.

We are going to analyze some particularly powerful hand moves: "steepling and hand-wringing" and "thumb displays."

Hand Steepling and Hand-Wringing

Hand steepling is one of the most potent signs of true confidence. Steepling involves touching or pressing the fingers of both hands in such a way that they are not interlacing, and the palms of the hands do not touch one another.

The gesture is referred to as steepling, as it resembles a church steeple's top. It conveys that you possess great confidence and that your thoughts, as well as position in the situation, are both solid and congruent. Steepling is both used to add empowerment to your delivery as well as command attention.

Hand wringing, on the other hand, suggests unease and discomfort. Hand wringing is the move where the fingers interlace, as though you were making a prayer gesture. One interesting thing is just how quickly somebody can go from steepling to hand wringing in the space of a few seconds, instantly conveying that there is a change in reaction or mood to something you just said or did.

To understand these two gestures, watch as many debates as you can catch; debates are often environments of high mental pressure, and you will very likely see people switch from steepling to hand wringing and then back again quite frequently you will be surprised.

Thumb Displays

The thumb is the one finger that stands out from the rest. It is a peculiar finger as well as the most important of them all. It has been explained countless times that without the thumb and all the little motions and twists that it makes possible; we would only now be breaking through the ceiling of the Stone Age. Think about this for a while to properly understand the power of the thumb. The peculiarity of the thumb has, since time immemorial, been a great way of human expression.

The thumbs-up move displays positivity and approval. In addition, when you pocket your hands but decide to leave the thumbs out, you are subconsciously communicating high confidence and a sense of relaxation.

On the other hand, tucking your thumbs into your pockets along with the rest of the hand may suggest that you are experiencing some negative emotions, or that you are significantly on edge. It can also mean it is below 30-degree weather, and you need to savor warmth anywhere accessible.

So, I bet you have learned quite a few things about body language and know how to read feet, arms and the torso to know what someone is communicating. In order to be a "guru" at reading body language, it is great to also understand deceptive body language. More on this in the following chapters.

Picking Up on Deceptive Body Language Behavioral Clusters

Before we evaluate the body language that you need to look out for to know if someone is trying to deceive you, let us attempt to understand why people try to be deception. There are many reasons why someone may want to be deceptive; however, these two are the primary ones:

- Persuasion
- Avoiding detection

If the context of the situation of your interaction with someone else involves any of these two, and what is described below keeps showing up in the other person's body language, it is very probable they are deceiving you.

A deceptive person is usually very concerned about being discovered for what they are and stand for. This concern, a lot of the time, shows:

Anxiety

Unless he or she is psychopathic or extremely good at acting, a deceptive person is typically anxious. As a result, they will send signals of tension. These may include sudden, jerky movements, sweating, minor muscle twitches, changes in the tone of voice, Etc. Note that with regard to minor muscle twitches, the muscles around the mouth and eyes are usually the most susceptible. Keep an eye for this to catch deception.

Control

In order to avoid getting caught, there will be varied signs of over-control. For instance, friendly body language will be forced and it will often appear too 'cultivated.' Look out for those smiles where the mouth smiles but the eyes do not smile, and by the way, this is not just something fancy people say: if the sides of the mouth crinkle but the sides of the eyes do not, this is a fake smile where the eyes do not smile.

The anxious person will also attempt to hold their body still in order to hide tell-tale signs. For instance, they may put their hands in their pockets. Another example is projecting their words with either limited or exaggerated emphasis.

Distracted

A person out to deceive usually needs to think in overdrive; they need to think way more about their activity than is normal. Thus, they may drift, mid-story, as they think of what they will say next. Watch for hesitations and random, unnatural pauses. Anxiety will also lead to such actions as fidgeting and paying attention to unusual places.

If you are enjoying this book, would you be kind enough to leave a review on Amazon because I would like to hear how the book has improved your life. If you make it to the last page of this book and did not enjoy its value, publisher details will be given to inform what could have been done to better serve your expectations.

Picking Up on Defensive Body Language Behavioral Clusters

When a person feels threatened in some way, they will take up defensive postures to try to defend themselves. Here are the basic defensive body language motions/responses:

Covering the vital organs/points of vulnerability

This one involves covering the torso, which we have already looked at. The chin is held down so that the neck is covered, and the groin is protected with either the knees together or legs crossed. It is an ancient human defense mechanism that still unfurls today, even in the complete absence of physical harm.

Fending off

The arms may be thrust out so as to fend off the 'attacker.' More likely though, is the more subtle curved-arms pose to deflect the hurt.

Using a barrier

Any physical item may be placed between the person and his addressor, so as to act as a literal, and more often, figurative barrier. The item could be a pen cap or a cabinet. Have you ever noticed some people calm down significantly when allowed to straddle a reversed chair?

Other examples of barriers are cushions hugged against the torso and teddy bears.

Becoming small

One way to defend against an attack is to minimize the target size. Thus, a person may huddle so that they occupy a smaller space, keeping both arms and legs pulled in.

Rigidity

This is yet another primitive response. The muscles tense up, making them harder, and this helps them withstand an attack better. Also, it freezes the body, minimizing movements that may attract the attention of the 'predator.' This one is a common feature in such primary feeders as gazelles and rabbits.

Hiding

This one is simple enough; a person who feels vulnerable seeks the safety of a safe space. For instance, you may walk on the inside part of the sidewalk, or away from the road. You may also observe somebody take up the farthest corner seat of a room.

Seeking escape

Eye flicking from one side to the other may show that the person is, often subconsciously, seeking a way out.

Pre-Empting the 'Attack'

Giving-in

The defensive person will adopt submissive body language, avoid looking into your eyes, keep his or her head down and perhaps crouch if the environment allows for it.

Attacking first

Aggressive body language may show up, as the person adopts the 'attack is the best defense form' mentality. Watch for an erect body and quick interjections. Better yet, watch for 'conflicting' body language. If the upper body is thrust out in aggressive fashion, but the legs are crossed/knees pressed together, the person is only exhibiting aggression because he/she is defensive.

Let us now move on to reading various emotions using your body language.

Picking Up on Emotional Body Language Behavioral Clusters

If you are a careful observer, you will be able to detect emotions from nonverbal signs. However, and this applies to the rest of the clusters covered in this book, these are primarily indicators with high accuracy levels and not absolute guarantees. Try to use contextual clues to read body language appropriately. Here are quick tips to help us look at some emotions and some non-verbal clues that will depict them:

Anger

- The face and neck are red or flushed
- Fists are clenched
- Teeth are bared
- Leaning forward is exhibited, and the invasion of body space

Fear, Anxiety and Nervousness

Fear usually occurs when basic needs are threatened. Seeing as fear has been around longer in human evolution than most other emotions, there are many levels of it, from mild anxiety to uncontrolled terror. Here are easy-to-detect bodily changes brought about by fear:

- A cold sweat

- A pale face
- A dry mouth: this one is often indicated by drinking water or merely licking the lips
- Damp eyes
- Erratic eye contact
- Trembling lower lip
- Voice tremors
- Errors of speech
- Visible high pulse
- Tension in muscles, indicated by clenched fists, jerky motions, legs wrapped around objects and elbows tucked to the sides
- Holding of breath and gasping
- Fidgeting
- Defensive body language, such as folded arms and crossed legs. Generally, limbs get drawn in, as opposed to being splayed.

Sadness

This is the opposite of happiness, and it is an indicator of a depressive state.

- Trembling lip
- Flat tone of speech
- Drooping of the body
- Tears

Embarrassment

This may be caused by either guilt or some transgression of values

- The neck and face are flushed
- Looking down or looking away from other people
- False smiling
- Grimacing, changing topics or making concerted attempts to cover up the embarrassment

Surprise

This one occurs when things were unexpected

- The eyebrows are raised
- Eyes widen
- Mouth hangs open
- Sudden retreating/backward movement

Happiness

- General muscle relaxation
- Genuine smiling
- Open body language, with the limbs stretched out and the torso exposed.

Body Language for Career Success

Now that you know the different kinds of body language and what they mean, what's next? Knowing how to read body language is practically worthless unless you use it real life, in situations that will benefit you greatly. And one type of situation where your newly acquired knowledge of reading body language is the area of business or career.

When it comes to doing business, you'll need to be very persuasive. The same goes for your career too if you're an employee instead of an entrepreneur. If you want to snag the biggest deal of your entrepreneurial life that can launch your business to a whole new level, you'll need to successfully convince your prospective client or customer that they will benefit the most if they choose to buy your products or hire your services. If you're looking to grow your business via joint ventures with very established businesses, you'll need to convince the owners of such businesses that their partnering with your company is their best bet to generate much more income. As an employee that wants to climb all the way to the top of the corporate ladder, you must be able to sell the idea that promoting you will be in the best interests of the department and the company as a whole to your immediate superiors and upper management. Without the ability to persuade and convince effectively, you won't get anywhere in business or your career.

Now that you've learned how to read body language, you are in much better position to optimize your chances of successfully persuading customers, clients, or superiors for your benefit. How?

If you can read the body language of others with great accuracy (not perfect accuracy because there's no such thing), you can plan your actions accordingly. And when you're able to do that, your chances of successfully convincing them to act in your favor will be much, much higher.

Another way that your newly acquired knowledge of body language will help you optimize your people-persuading success is by being able to employ the appropriate body language signals to subtly and effectively communicate your ideas to them. Remember, there's a saying that effective communications is 10% verbal and 90% non-verbal. If you're able to project the appropriate body language signals while interacting with current and potential business prospects and your superiors, the 90% of your ability to effectively communicate with them becomes much higher.

How Does It Look

Let's say you're an entrepreneur whose business is an online content managing one. Your business helps other entrepreneurs and even big businesses establish a strong online presence through which their products and services can be promoted. Such an online presence includes putting up a website, managing it, and drawing people to that website.

Imagine that you're pitching your content management agency services to one of your city's biggest restaurants that wants to grow their business even more through the internet. This is your moment to establish your agency as one of the top in your state simply because of the status of this prospective client. How do you use your knowledge of body language to optimize your chances of getting them as your client?

It begins with the way you walk into the room. If you walk slowly and head held high instead of hurriedly and looking down, you're communicating to them that you're confident about yourself and, by extension, what you're about to offer them. And if they see that you're confident, they'll be more open to what you will present. Also, a slower, steadier pace exhibits preparedness and non-neediness. There is no quality more magnetizing than a person who wants but does not need.

Next, communicate your confidence and competence even more with your posture as you begin to present. Assuming the spread-legs standing position together with an open-chested position where your arms are at the sides and palms exposed can send the subtle signal that you're confident about what you're presenting and that you're trustworthy (not hiding anything). So, even as you're just starting your pitch, you can subtly communicate to your prospects that they can trust you, i.e., you're very capable and honest. You have now made a very good first impression.

While first impressions are crucial and lasting, you'll need to sustain the good impression that you've started. The next step is to establish a good rapport with your audience. And one of the most effective body languages for establishing rapport is good eye contact during your presentation and when they're asking you questions. When you maintain good eye contact, you communicate several important things, namely:

- That you're personally communicating to them and you're not just talking to the air;

- That they're important since, through eye contact, you're acknowledging their presence;

- That what their saying is interesting and important to you (how do you feel when you're talking to someone who doesn't look at you in the eye?); and

- You aren't deceiving them (remember that lack of eye contact can also communicate an ongoing attempt to deceive or hide something).

At one point in my life there was a man who approached me in a retail store and asked me about my occupation. He was nice but seemed awfully nervous. I figured I'd overlook it because he was offering me a chance to discuss business opportunities when I was trying to find ways to build network connections. However, things became a bit too weird for my liking. Every time we met, I repeatedly asked him what he was offering. His answers always were vague and somewhat related to the response of, "My wife and I know some great people who helped us make a lot money". Sounds nice, but the details were lacking. He had spiels, pitches, and stories to draw a person's attention. Here's where he messed up, I was not so desperate for networking opportunities to become blind to the fact that his eye contact and body language were deceitful. Have you ever met someone and knew something was just "off"? That's the feeling I felt, and it was stronger than ever. While discussing business and answering his questions about my goals, there was a nervous energy that covered the dialogue. Any person continually showing signs of nervousness after meeting in-person three times is an instant red flag! Furthermore, every time we stopped discussing business, his tone of voice became relaxed and normal. So, I decided to decline any further meetings as my intuition told me that this guy was trying to recruit me for some kind of multi-level marketing or pyramid scheme. Trust your gut when meeting new people. There is always another person or opportunity right around the corner if you "miss out".

Another way you can start building rapport between you and your prospects is through an open body position, i.e., your arms do not cover your torso and are on the side to expose the upper body and your hands aren't hidden in your pockets. Covering your torso by crossing your arms in front of your chest can communicate to other people that you're looking down on them or that you're not open to what they may ask or say to you. And both can make your prospects feel disconnected from you on a personal level, which can minimize your chances of successfully pitching your agency's services.

Rapport is very important because of what master salesman and Guru Tom Hopkins said about the human nature of buying: "People buy emotionally and justify the purchase logically." This means if you want to optimize your chances of making sales or closing deals, then you'll need to appeal to the heart more than the mind. And rapport is an emotional thing, not a logical one because it's a feeling of being connected to the other person.

When your prospects' hearts start to open up to you, it means they are now receptive to what you're saying. The so-called emotional barriers start to be removed, paving the way for you to convince them to hire your content management agency for their business.

Lastly, you can use nods, hand and arm gestures, changing facial expressions, and a genuine smile (which includes smiling of the eyes) to effectively emphasize what you're communicating to your prospects. This is important because it shows that you're not rigid, which we discussed earlier as a pre-emptive and defensive body language.

Next, you'll need to figure out whether or not what you're doing is working. This is where reading the body language of your prospect comes into play. He or she may not verbalize what's going on inside his heart and mind, but chances are, signals can be picked up via gestures, posture, and facial expressions. And if you're able to promptly catch these signals with relatively high accuracy, you will be in a very good position to proceed accordingly, i.e., continue what you're doing or do something different.

Let's say that while doing your pitch, you observe that the owner of the restaurant is holding down his head and he's crossing his arms in front of his chest. It highly possible that your pitch isn't working in terms of persuading him to get your agency's services. He may have serious concerns about what you're presenting or worse, he's become utterly unimpressed by you and your service. Through these signals, you can change gears and take appropriate actions.

One such action is pausing your presentation to ask the restaurant owner if he has any questions or concerns at this point in your presentation. To do this, you must be able to ask the right questions in order to draw out what's really on the restaurant owner's mind concerning either you or your services. If you're not able to do this, you won't be able to address his concerns and consequently, your chances of convincing him to engage your agency's services are very low. But if you can successfully draw out his true concerns or objections, then you'll know how to proceed with the pitch and minimize the risk for a failed pitch.

Through this example, I hope you now have a more advanced understanding of body language, i.e., how you can use such knowledge to advance in your career as an entrepreneur or employee. Next, we'll talk about how you can use your body language knowledge to win in your personal relationships.

Body Language and Relationship Success

While success in one's career is one of the most satisfying things a person can experience in his life, it won't mean much without meaningful, satisfying, and intimate personal relationships. All the monetary success in the world won't mean much without people to share them with. Fortunately, you can also use knowledge of body language to make your most important personal relationships even more intimate and meaningful.

When you're able to read the body languages of the most important people in your life with relatively high accuracy, you can have insights as to what's really going on inside their hearts and minds. And when you know such things, you will know how to best interact with them at the moment.

How Does It Look

Let's say your teen-age daughter accidentally broke your highly-cherished coffee mug after you left for work. And this mug isn't just a mug to you but one of your most cherished memories of your deceased mother. She used to give you your coffee in the morning before going to university – and later on, to work. That's why you highly cherish this mug.

You come home just in time for family dinner. You see your daughter, you say "Hi, Twinky Pops!" and wait for her to give you the customary hug and kiss every time you come home. But you notice something but can't put a finger on what it is. While you can't exactly figure what it is, your teenaged daughter was acting anxiously, i.e., her tone of voice seemed way less perky and she doesn't establish eye contact. She was also acting quite controlled, i.e., "reserved" and "cultured" at the dinner table and when she smiled when you told the family about your promotion earlier in the day, her smile seemed hollow or fake (only the lips and not the eyes).

With all of these body language signs, you can deduce that something's bothering her. And if you're cognizant of body languages and how to use them in your personal relationships, you know that acting normally towards her won't cut it if you want to help her.

After reading her body language and deducing that something is bothering her, you want to know what that is and – if it's within your power – help her. But if you want to be able to successfully convince her to open up to you and tell you the truth, you will also need to use appropriate body language that will communicate to her that she can be vulnerable with you without being punished for it, i.e., emotional security. How do you do that?

After asking to speak with her alone in her bedroom, you can employ a genuinely smiling face (take the effort to smile with the eyes too), establish and maintain eye contact, keep your torso open (don't cross your arms across your chest to communicate that you are open to whatever she has to say), don't cross your legs, and touch or tap her on the arm as a gesture of reassurance that, whatever it is, you'll listen and will not get mad. It will greatly help if you also use a calm and gentle tone of voice. As she talks, you can nod your head slightly to express that you get what she's saying and that you're genuinely listening to her.

And the coup de grace when she finally drops the bomb on what really happened, i.e., she broke your cherished coffee mug, you can either touch her arms gently or hug her while saying "Oh, Sweetie, you're more important to me than that mug." after she apologizes. Through a gentle tone of voice and appropriate body language, you can communicate to her that she can be vulnerable with you because with you, she's emotionally safe. Your relationship with your teenage daughter can become even more intimate after this because you were able to effectively communicate to her that you love her and that she can be vulnerable with you with your body language.

Conclusion

This book has taught you quite comprehensively about body language. Everything you have picked up will be essential in helping you take in other people's body language and analyze it correctly.

However, a book is often never enough. You need to apply yourself. Train for this: go outside and interact with other people. Look at them and take in how they respond. Then hold their responses against the material gleaned here and see if you progressively advance in the art of body language reading. Always remember: contextual clues are very important. Always keep context in mind as you read body language. Refer back to this book before and after your interactions to effectively craft your social awareness.

Please remember to leave your review on Amazon if you enjoyed this book. Thank you and always strive to continue growing!